Gnomon

AyPress

Ann Marie Yeager

"So, (sigh), uh, tea?""

AyPress
3546 Steubenville Rd., SE
Amsterdam, OH 43903

AyPress and its colophon ("lions guarding
sun") are trademarks of Aypress.

Published and Printed in the United States
of America.

AyPress website: www.aypress.com

Library of congress Catalogue-in-Publication
Data: Yeager, Ann Marie, 1966-;
1. Philosophical Verse   I. Title   II. Author
2003093964

First Edition, Hardcover

ISBN: 0-9742582-1-0

1 11 22 33 44 55 66 77 88 99

Distributed to the trade by Ingram

Gnomon, Greek,: "Interpreter."

—*Random House Webster's*
College Dictionary ©1992, pg. 570

Chapters:

I. "So (sigh), uh, tea?"

(Infers society prefers to bypass conversations, which could turn heated, believing politeness is proper etiquette. Such conversations are the breeding grounds for cultivating growth.)
   Discusses education, religion, government, legislation, statesmanship, penal conduct, racism, materialism.

II. In the Halls of Eternity:

Love, ascribed in elegant, and wistful tones, by the sighs of a romantic.

III. "Wee'ds":

Ideals to elevate children, and the child within.

IV. To Walk On Stars:

(A reference to the dead placed in constellations.) Lamentations on suicide, death, and society's ideals on death.

V. Eco, Echo, & Ego:

Man in his environment; self-improvement; audacity; speech, language; and health.

Excerpts from *Need I Say 'More.'*

"The poet, with the adjustment of a phrase, with the contrast of an image, with the rhythm of a line, has fixed a focus, which all the talk, and all the staring of the world, has been unable to fix before him. His is a labor which is at all times necessary, for without it, that sense of human reality, which is the poet's greatest accomplishment, is lost."

—Archibald Macleish

"Axioms in philosophy—are not axioms, until they are proved upon our pulses. We read fine things, but never feel them to the full—until we have gone the same steps of the author."   —John Keats

"Learned men, in all ages, have had their judgment free (and most, commonly disagreeing) from the common judgment of the world.

...Plato...condemned—many things that were maintained in the world, and required many things to have been reformed...

I am content to do—in uprightness of heart, and with a testimony of good conscience."

—John Knox

"For all men strive to grasp what they do not know; while none strive to grasp what they already know; and all strive to discredit what they do not excel in, while none strive to discredit what they do excel in. This is why there is chaos."   —Chuang Tzu
[369-286 BC]

"The scholar only knows how dear these silent, yet eloquent, companions o f pure thoughts and innocent hours, become—in the season of adversity."
—Washington Irving

"...In all things, endeavor to act on principle, and do not live like the rest of mankind, who pass through the world, like straws upon a river, which are carried which way the stream or wind drives them..."
—Susana Wesley {Letter to her son;
dated Epworth, October, 1709}

"A little philosophy—inclineth man's mind to athesim, but depth in philosophy—bringeth men's minds about to religion."   —Francis Bacon

"Come, follow me—and leave the world to its babblings."   —Dante

"So, (sigh), uh—tea?"

Masters' Lesson: CXVl {116}

Philosophy is like food.
One digests its content, but wastes—
what cannot read'ly absorb.

By steady consumption of,
grad'lly, the bits and pieces build,
become part of conscious mind.

Llanterns of Caterpillars:

Con-scious, (-*shes*, like *shhh!*):
    silent manipulation,
  of thought battling thought.

Llanterns of Caterpillar: Confutable

That which needs selling—
is confutable to soul,
from food to people.

Confutable means "prove to be false; bring to
nothing." There is a difference between "awareness" and
"selling." Selling is redundant desperation. This haiku was
worked to contain "four" words each line.

Masters' Lesson: CCXII {222}

Not one of us belongs here; all from othe' place.
When state, 'I feel out of place' (in social scene),
convey, 'out of comfort with experience.'
Comfort is acceptance of mentality.

"So,(sigh), uh, tea?"

Masters' Lesson: XCVII {97}

"Change," in one, does not constitute "growth," in one.
"Change" can occur on a horizontal line,
but a horizontal line, does not arise.

Horizontal can be broken into "hor" (time) + "|"
(self) + "zon" (zone). Thus, men define age—as a number
(time written as numbers), rather than growth of mentality.

Rue 'ems

A mere house—does not represent a mere individual.
Many—live in the guise of one house.
Man calls those divisions: "rue-'ems" (rooms).

A Rotten Disposition

How sweet the trees, when they die:
floral musk, peat'd moss, cedar sighs;
a final ode, a fading smile,
a long-fond, farewell wave—
to bequeath the Earth, a gift *"bough-tied"*
for *"e-turn-all"* support it gave.

If man but smelled, half as sweet,
in what state of grace, happ'ly lies;
in tree abode, in words of I'll,
in soul the size of stave;
how befitting 'ttribute, when man dies—
he just stinks in the isolate grave.

Masters' Lesson: CCXXIII {223}

When tree is cut down, and reshaped to purpose,
does not lose strength, perseverance, endurance.
One slice can support great weight, for centuries.
Man is like a tree; words reconstruct his would.

Masters' Lesson: XXXIV {34}

Tree man most admires—aged tree ope'd to full bloom.

Trees in forest jab one another with limbs.

Forest reflects men in hist'ry and city.

Onl' tree unprodded, grows to fullest p'tential.

Masters' Lesson: LXXV {75}

For one to ridicule a questioning mind,
is to applaud spite, and merit ignorance.
There exists no one ignorant, or stupid.
There are only minds—willed, or not—to learn.

Masters' Lesson: CCXXIV {224}

Education—not in how a building looks.
Brick, mortar: met'phors; build mind to higher heights.
Institutions concerned with appearances—
but interested in producing facades.

Lessons of the Five:

"Log-ick"

"Cycle-logical"—
creates and impacts
"socio-log'cal."

Masters' Lesson: CCXXV {225}

Only thought one ever learns—thought of another;
 A thought that's easily upset—is not true.
 Truth will withstand battery of all questions
 without containing contradiction, or holes.

Masters' Lesson: X {10}

Ignorance—is a closed mind,
suppression of society,
believing it has learned truth.

"Knowledge, without integrity, is dangerous and dreadful.
—Samuel Johnson

"If a little knowledge is dangerous—where is the man, who has so much, as to be out of danger?"
—T. H. Huxley

"His—had been an intellectual decision, founded on his conviction, that if a little knowledge was a dangerous thing—a lot—was lethal."
—Tom Sharpe

Masters' Lesson: CCXXVI {226}

It is not knowledge—that is dangerous,
but the ignorance, which still remains.
Knowledge does not constitute *wisdom*.

Lessons of the Five:
Cycles, or "Psych-L's"
{L representing "angles"}

Doubt foreshadows faith.
Faith foreshadows Truth.
Truth foreshadows doubt.

"So, (sigh), uh, tea?"

Masters' Lesson: CXXXI {131}

Each belief contains word lie.
Lie as in falsehoods, untruths; or—
as potential not yet tapped.

Compounded Preclusion

"Poet Erza Pound (born in Hailey, Idaho) left
America for Europe.

Some of his early Cantos expressed contempt
towards American politicians and economists;

'Following the worldwide depression of the 1930s,
he turned more and more to history, especially economic
history...Between 1941 and 1943, after Italy and the
United States were at war, he made several hundred
broadcasts over Rome Radio, often openly condemning the
U.S. war effort.'

He was arrested by U.S. forces in 1945, and
spent six months in a prison camp near Pisa." Pound, at age
sixty, was brought to Washington to stand trial for treason
in May, 1945.

'He was pronounced 'insane and mentally unfit for
trial' by a panel of doctors, and spent 12 years (1946-58)
in St. Elizabeth's Hospital for the criminally insane, in
Washington, D.C. '

After he was released, he returned to Italy (where
he died: November 1, 1972).

Pound won the Bolligen Prize for *The Pisan
Cantos*, written in that Pisa prison camp."

-Merriam Webster's Encyclopedia of Literature, and
A Treasury of Great Poems.}

Erza: Razed

At sixty, Pound, for Pound, was tried unsound;
Thus, I ask—what is an un-*sound* word?
The coinage pre-*scribes,* "no voice is heard,"
Thus, wit must be lost in listeners' *crown* ;
For men, who do not study breath of pen,
Proclaim by ear, trained to listen to chain,
that another, who thinks outside that chain,
"posses" thought that threatens their ought of men,
(which they proclaim is for humanity).

Humanity or humility?
How things look different across the "see."
Only men, who lead men, eradicate men:
who expose truth of their corrupt action.

If U.S. is comprised of diversity,
How can *diff'rent*—be called "crimin'lly."

"I am mortified to be told,
that in the United States of America,
the sale of a book—can become a subject of inquiry,
and of criminal inquiry, too."
—Thomas Jefferson

Son-net: Trappings

{Law-awed laud flawed,
by applaud allowed,
a loud load to lode the odd.}

Men are whores—to other men:
Conditioned to accept, without questionin';
Without care as to how their acts æffect,
From war to religion, to work and sex;
Without searching for the reason why—
They fight to uphold their beliefs by;
From school'd, to church, to government,
They learn to conform by punishment.
Thus, men are whores to other men,
Because they fear ridicule, bein' condemn'd.
Ask a man why he does what he does,
He'll answer in drone of "so-sigh-tea" fuzz.

If you were never taught—what taut to believe,
Would you follow a thought— were taught to seethe?

What affects, effects.

"Trea-son": Crucifixion

{Gal. 3:13: "Christ...(became) a curse...for cursed is
everyone, who is hung on a tree." [Trea-]}

There can be no such thing as treason,
For there is no such thing as government!
There are only men—who convene, cement,
By *"row-tating"* minds of "I'm's" in season;
Where each, by own will, egotistick'lly reason—
That their own morals—are the implements,
To cure other men's problem'd increments,
By *"compounded sentences"* increasin'.

Then, those men die (or, are ousted by vote),
And law becomes *stool* for new turn *cote*;*
Where new—eradicate—past morals laud,
Enact their own voice of earthen god.
Thus, what is called *"treason"*—is reci'tive,
For law and governments change by 'lective.

*Stool Pigeon

Rime: "I-Ooze-Shun

A man can put on a suit and tie,
To words he speaks, both sly and wry,
And convince a slew, and connive a few,
Ingrate he's great at puppeting, too!
And win an election, a delegation,
To herald affection, congrad'lation:
Campaign, champagne; order, or do ordain;
But the infest'tion question that remains:
The words he rent, before convent
(A sat'ration of irr'tation, ind'gnation:
Accused opponents, confused proponents)—
Will he not abuse, use "you's" from legis' pews?
A man is a man in any position;
Not delegate, but relegate self-mission.

The Town "At-torn-ey" of Millstone
{Or, "Sit-ee"" Ordain-nance"}

["Professional pet sitter (name)...rushed to the aide
of friends, during tropical storm 'Floyd'...'Animals were
dying; people were calling me in tears; hysterical that they
didn't want to abandon their pets; begging me to come get
them.' She round-up, fed, cleaned, treated, and then found
temporary homes for the animals...and was issued a summons
for violating zoning ordinance—for operating a temporary
animal shelter...a fine up to $1,000."
—AP; The Repository (Canton, OH) 11-23-99}

Yes! Man must have a _permit_ to act nice!
God knows we wouldn't want to demonstrate—
That laws are examples of tolerates;
Where men can help men, without charging price,
Or set the prec'dence of kindlier vice.
Thus, laws, for solution, were not to state,
But serve moral rectitude self-creates.
That man must pay a man to 'l_low_ a man— is an _"Off-ice."_
That man must babysit man on Earth,
Makes infants of men, in moral cure'th!
The intolerance disguised—is chastised _"act-shun,"_
To _"pen-all-eyes"_ and _"scrut-in-l's"_: _"at-tension."_

There is only one cure for intolerance,
That is to rid the self of insolence.

40

Rime of Abbey Seed

(To Worship Production of Tangible)

"Money doesn't grow on trees," many quip;
    (Indignant at living desire today).
"*Act-u-all-y*" does, but not allowed to play,
By col'ring paper-pulp—with own encrypt'.
'Tis h*on-or-off*ered system, men but stip';
    (Thus thief honors stupidity, when retrieves—
For *"stays"* within *"con-fines"* that men believe:
A tree's no val*ue*, 'til cut to blue chip).
Do men believe the soul cannot achieve,
Unless starved or manip'lated *"to pay?"*
Then why take land (thus food) from job reprieved?
'Tis keeping dreams aggrieved, by body's bray.

    If worry o'er money in bank, on hand—
    Possess no talent for tomorrow's stand.

Stip': stipulation.

Master's Lesson: CCXXVII {227}

Money was invented to manipulate.
A starved man—will ex'cute a fed man's bidding.
Money—is word, "one," centered in the word, "my."
What's val'ble to keep in life? Life extends b'yond.

Masters' Lesson: CCXXVIII {228}

Talent stems from having trained.
The gift—is the urge—to perform.
Ev'rything else up to you.

Masters' Lesson: CXLIII {143}

The only thing broken pottery can do—
is to evoke the'ries and sustain questions.
Archaeology should be a dig through tomes.

From Hysteri' to History: New Millenniums
[For future generations]

The end of *"were-old"*–is n'er the end of earth;
    Refers to change in way one thinks to act,
    This date that worries minds to panic: *fact!*
Each man is a world, "a-part" formed at birth,
    Lim'ted to *eyes*, as long as *I's* endur'th;
And year to year, one changes gradu'l tact,
    As mind's alt'ring theory, for truth extract:
Rev'lations: "Illum'*Nations*," robbing mirth.

    How many times—have millenn'ums past?
    How many people prophesied doom?
And still, the earth and man contin'e to last.
All these predictions, people just assume.

"Thou—sands" of years, are bottled, blanched tears,
    That irritate *eyes* to cleanse with ears.

Hysteri': Hysteria

Masters' Lesson: XXI {21}

The forward thrust of a thought—is a problem.
A thought thrust beyond problem—is solution.
Like a made road, a thought—also has an end.
Each problem has root; Roots branch; Roads: ought of line.

["Pro Bállein," Greek root of "*problem*"; means "to throw."]

Llanterns of Caterpillars:
"Eye-I": Via-a-Vie

Via a problem,
one becomes mob'ler (by use)—
inserting the "eye."

["*Mob'ler*" begins *mob* (that is, the collective, not
the individual). Its letters are extracted from the word,
"problem," less the letter p. *Mob'ler* is *mobiler* (to move
fluidly, unencumbered), but the individual must insert the "i "
(eye), ability to envision.]

"Prop-he-cies" (sees):

[The Legacy of Men Who Want Revenge,
For How Each Felt While Here.]

Prophecies are "pro-feces," scribed in shat;
A fear logic'lly planted in mind's palette.
If Nostradamus predicted peace,
Would we prepare for war, or look for reas'?

Nostra Damnatus, Latin: "our own guilt,"
Thus, professed intent in name he built.
For actions that men made his father bear,
He creat'd revenge, by use of hist'ry's ear.

Even Rev-elations 'ttempts to give us doom,
(So much for men of faith; 'tis faith of fume!).
It seems to me, psychological ploys,
Tell man his future's threatened, man destroys.

Prop-he-cies are revenge 'tolled for action,
By planting reverse psych'log'cal prediction.

{Tell a man what he'll be, he'll create mental'toy.}

Reas': Reason; Mental'toy: toy with mentality. 'Tolled:
Extolled. Greek myths teach above: Zeus & father.

47

"So,(sigh), uh, tea?"

Masters' Lesson: LXIV {64}

The'ry of evolution is based on change;
yet, man's the an'mal, who can't stand be diff'rent.
He competes to be the same—not is'lated.
We're not shaped by gen'tics, but what we admire.

48

Masters' Lesson: CXLV {145}

Mora is Latin for *fool.*
Moral, then, is the fool's angle.
Angles can't see whole æffect.

One cannot expect to build a nation on death,
without its citizens—e'er remaining in the firm belief,
that death—is the solution to all their problems.

Masters' Lesson: LVII {57}

That which opens—learns and gains.
That which closes—ignorance stains.
That not changed—stagnation drains.

"So,(sigh), uh, tea?"

Llanterns of Caterpillars: "F-ear"

To close one's self off—
is to be controlled.
To open, is to control.

{"In a civilized society..."}

Civilize—phonetics, "one must sieve out the lies" from the truth.

Civil—is but a bunch of Roman Numerals— merged together as a habitat (100-4-150).

Thus, *civilized*: merely the number of those eyes—watching each other.

Masters' Lesson: LXXXII {82}

<u>Mental</u>'ty's comprised of <u>men</u>:
the <u>tally</u> of thoughts in one's mind,
<u>why</u>'d-ened 'gainst own ideas.

Stagnation is only hindrance to equating progress.
Is not progress also made—by moving backward?

Riddle Me—This Conundrum...

{Conundrum: A riddle, whose answer involves a pun.}

They say that comets are made of ice,
(yet, who has touched the bright-nomad star?)
Not star, diff'rent, "bigger bun, meteor."
(yet, 'tis same mol'cule from near to far.)

Light travels this distance in one year.
(yet, whose eyes have held that interest stare.)
Deep space has diamonds; voids o' black holes.
(yet, who among us has traveled there.)

{Who can catch the end of light,
and who can stand on air;
Who can catch a shooting star,
and who can disappear.}

The earth's core is this temperature.
(Whose fingertips have felt its abyss?)
Man evolved from existing monkeys.
('Tis hypoth'sis of _paren_thesis!)

{They squint their eyes, synopsize,
boldly adjusting specks;
while an object at five feet—
a microscope corrects!

55

With cry-vocals, bi-focals,
who can but truly see;
what is it we learn of "truth"—
'cept man makes misery.

"F Act" d'rides, and equates not truth;
'tis 'bbreviation: "f(iction) act";
as hist'ry's invent'd mouth-to-mouth,
con-s(c)ent'd by ex-perts "dumb-found'd" pact.

Who can recant, what planet decants,
as if anything here, was/is new;
everything was made æons ago,
is same energy, or residue.

As soil's matter made the seed,
and seed loomed cotton weed;
then cotton stitched long-sleeved shirt:
new shirt is as old as dirt.

The *beautiful* Danann word *eevin*,
Catholics have rewrote Æ bhinn.
If there is diff'rence in just a word—
what truth to cultures o'erheard?

Why do they school-preach these Ologies—
to train young minds—'tis fact!
When 'tis all merely *theory* cast:
A science-fiction pact.}

[We've fallen from the Tower,
where first monks rose to power;
offsprung our mind from his chest,
now 'tis quiet in the "fore-st."

All the "monk-ees" listening,
to the one that sounds the best:
One "monk-ee" grunting louder,
deeper above the rest.

Hear him cry: *"-ie," "-ee"*
Infantile mentality.
That's man's origin of history:
"Monk-ees"—from religion tree.]

What is "forest," and "first," but "forced."

Masters' Lesson: LXXXVIII {88}

Chopping down a "Christmas" tree,
watching it slowly bleed to death—
is like crucifying Christ.

To crown with mocking heaven,
on crossed stand; weigh limbs with objects;
teach glee of death with "gimmes."

Mocking the Hypocrisy
o' Their Philosophy

I smiled and chatted with a man I knew,
a man, the church-going crowd would eschew.
APPALLED! Casting critical eye,
said, "he's a drunk, drug-stealing lie!"
and I *SHOULD NOT!* converse with such a shrew!

I looked at them, in stern mocking disdain,
with el'quent 'ophy, started to explain,
"You say God forgives—any crime,
with open arms—at any time,
and yet—with your forgiveness—you refrain."

"Here is soul-and-shell, just like you and I,
though makes different choices—I don't deny.
Since you talk of being God-like,
I must remind you of your psych':
'God doesn't turn His back on him—why should I?"

{'Ophy is short for "philosophy," while accent-
uating the thought, "oh, fie!" (disgust)}

"Can't –os" I: Stuck In The Middle of Rime

["...37 Tibetan Organizations urged India's
government to allow the 14-yr-old Karmapa to remain in
India (after fleeing China-ruled Tibet)..."
                    —Beacon Journal (A-3) 1-25-00]

What's gov'ment concerned with, but lording thought.
Afraid minds might astray minds, with Faust as foulst.
(Thus, why so much money's spent on guns to oust,
And "Agin-seize" for "ney-shuns" a sponsored spot).
Is flag a flog—to banner-banter speech?
With "dei-see-shuns" by few men's fumin' "a-liens,"
On "sit-a-zens" souls for ruler's careens?
What sod does swear allegiance men do preach?

Ah, r'legion must be more powe'ful than State;
Might quell the "vie-lense" generals create;
And by "eye-dia" path—to 'love not hate,'
May wizen "sold-jure" to leave his "gait."

Yea, Earth might uniform shell and soul;
But when its dirt has passed, you see the toll.

"So, (sigh), uh, tea?"

Masters' Lesson: CXVIII {118}

Institution puts *sty* in *intuition.*

Intuition—is built-in payment for soul.

Others can't earn pay—if they don't make one fear.

"Can't –os" II: "Mess-Eye, Uh":

If *"E-Manual"* came back to this wr<u>ought</u>—
Would you expect Him to work for money?
And how would you know one was that reve'ry?
Do you expect one to espouse the same thought,
Decantered in Bible, sep'rate from *Lot*?
What point would be return's necessity?
If *"By-Bell's"* *"test'ment"* is worded truthfully—
As 'lieve already have the wisdom sought.

Thus, any "r'turning"—to dispute what "truth"
These facets argue as religious couth;
Who seek the same: a name, a sign o' sain,
To uphold adjectives, over souls to reign.

"Gesus" is the hope of rescue by slaves.
Yet, "part-ici-pay-shun" chains men's ways.

[Ge (or Je) is Greek for "Earth." (A pronunciation near Egyptian "Giza," or Latin "Gaius.") "Ge-Henna" in Hebrew, means "hell"; literally means "valley of the son of Hinnom." Irish "De hAoine," (pronounced "je haynya; akin "ge henna") means "Friday." Friday, oddly, is named for the Norse God of love, Freya. Close to Frigg, the queen of Asgard, which is "the home of the gods." Hina, in Sanskrit, "means" "lesser, inferior." Gesus, probably means, "save from life/work (slavery) of hell."]

62

Masters' Lesson: XIII {13}

This fight o'er scripturous right:
Care not more—for ink on the page—
than for God's souls in each shell.

"Can't –os" |||:   "Firing Canons"
(Confusion of Sects with Sex)

["Sister...: 'Jesus was open to dialogue with anyone; including
people with whom he vehemently disagreed.'...We Are The
Church...members... called on the Vatican to approve ordination of
women; drop its requirements that priests remain celibate; and recognize
the human rights of gays and lesbians...In Denver, Former Archbishop
(name) banned the group from Church property."
—Repository (D-4) 2-17-97]

There is "dissi-dence" within one church,
For there is no recognition of God.
Merely thought—from man, that men have lawed,
As religion chirped at each <u>harpy</u> perch.

There, Pope, "too," r'cants the soul's but its shell,
That men are their genitals, nothing more;
As another "Past-or" looks at "Judges, Four":
Cites, "Deb'rah led Israel," thus, gender quell.

The wisdom to lead, does not arise from thighs,
But composure of mind, compassion of heart.
What Apostles meant, here <u>synopsize</u>:
The M.E. soci'ty deafen women "a—<u>part</u>."

"Spirit-chew-ow-tees" between one and God.
Cannot be severed by men's thoughts on bod'.

Masters' Lesson: LXIII {63}

Whosoe'er upholds state of equality,
must honor <u>all</u> in its definition, else—
'tis merely subjugated to one's ego.

Subjugate: "to bring under complete control; master;
enslave."

Masters' Lesson: CXXVI {126}

One, who thinks that another—
is only "good for one thing,"
has but one thought—with which to think.

7/7/8 ("screwed up")

"Can't-os" IV: "Die-sigh-pulls"

{"*Murder is a horrible sin; however—when a person accepts Jesus as their personal savior, they are forgiven and cleansed by the blood of Jesus... Your past sins are washed away...*"

—Pastor "C"; *Repository*}

So go ahead, murder. There is no shame.
The Bible's full of death, given in "*name.*"
Gi'e death to enemy—a holy rite,
"*To beat and trample in dust, with might.*"

Just kill; ask "pre'st's" forgiveness, kill again;
As long as ask *"for-giveness"*—it's no sin.
Thus, man's name for religion: is death,
To kill off the spirit, and unique breath.

An act obtain'd is mental entrainment;
It teaches soul its toll: how r'spond on cues.
The problem: Leaders' betters 'llow eschews.
N'er seek the ways of wiser implement.

No wonder the world's a blood-bath show;
The Church says "forgive act," but not forgo.

Masters' Lesson: CVIII {108}

Man writes his days with minus, division signs.
For every day lives, does he lessen self?
What day is today, when no longer a man?

(8-18-66; 8/18/66)

"Can't-os" V: "Disc(h)ord

["The aim is not to build a mosque; the aim is to (create) discord. That—is what we are against.'—Roman Catholic Patriarch (name), regional authority in "Holy Land." [To protest the building of a mosque (on a 1/3 of a 1/2 an acre) near the Basilica in Nazareth. The Vatican opted to close its Church doors—4 weeks before Christmas in Nazareth, Jerusalem, Bethlehem, and Galilee. The Patriarch indirectly confirmed that Church Leaders pressured Palestinian Government to intercede with the Islamic Movement."] 11/23 & 11/26-99] —Beacon Journal (Akron, OH)

A cult that isn't biased? Prej'dic'tic farce!
It isn't discord'c can'n? "Crew-saids" upheld;
To silence freed'm o' tongues, thus thousands felled.
It isn't discord? "No'then" Ireland's parse—
Where Cath'lic verses Protestant—prey by arse'.
'Tis discord "sored"—to denounce a spirit—
One's right to honor God—how one fere's it.
This Church against a Church makes slaves and marse.

When example 'legion sets—is expulsion,
Do not teach tol'rance, but repulsion.
To praise self amen—and raze soul o' men,
But seeks to punish, d'ssect, by belief defends.

If Church shows pettiness o'er Jesus, God—
It profits on what its ego applauds.

Masters' Lesson: XVII {17}

If one is close to God in mind and in heart,
one does not need to walk in the footsteps of—
institutions, who preach the fear of God's name.

"Can't-os" VI: Phooe'd or "Toil-et"

{"...If a man or woman refuses to work, the Bible
tells us not to even associate with this person...when a
person is simply lazy, the Bible instructs us not to feed, or
help them financially. We are to work, in order to be able to
feed ourselves..."   —"Pastor C", Repository 11-25-97}

'Tis stated, "what sep'rates man from an'mals—
Is gift to think; so is work not thought?
Yet, what does "past-or" do but repeat plot?
A life of fat-lounging on other men's brows.

'Tis man who invented money and rude,
And man who made man earn food.
'Tis man who prefers slave systems of hate,
These three things God did not create.
To criticize others with bridled brain,
Action's not like Jesus', more like Cain's.

No wonder world will never love impart,
E'er confined to decrepit insanity.
As Church, e'er late, to change its heart,
Is anchor d'taining man from human'ty.

God lent planet, with its bounty of food;
Onl' man misers its *can*—with leers, sells it subdued.

"So,(sigh), uh, tea?"

Masters' Lesson: 00 *(The Oughts)*

Ignore the rabble of men,
who preach the trust of God's life plan,
from behind bulletproof glass.

"Can't-os" VII: "Paul-Bearers":
Grim "Re-purse?"

Why do men believe not connected to God?
That souls need a liaison for ears on sod;
That other men are better, due to words
As if el'quent speaking, God treats preferred.

This "need a connection," gives soul a death;
Like those Egypt slaves, make rulers deith;
Believed were nothing, and must be guid'd;
Rewards incarnation, if priests abid'd.

What is a priest? Is he not merely man.
Susceptible to fallacies, no better than.
Church warns, don't speak with spirits, other side;
Yet what is God—but Spirit—on othe' side.

God speaks to each man in his own soul;
Through dream and gut, the voice for role.

{Is man savage—because of his religion?}

"So, (sigh), uh, tea?"

Masters' Lesson: CCXXIX {229}

Man has only persecuted one thing: Thought.
To grat'fy or rat'fy position in mind.
All problems' root: Belief control—way to peace.
Peace only obtained by truth—which affects all.

Masters' Lesson: CLXXXVII {187}

God, man d'clares as one syll'ble.
Satan separated in two:
disassociating with souls.

7/7/8

"Can't-os" VIII: "Rome-eo" and "Julius"

What's in religion? that, which call in vain—
By glor'ous self, enchanting homage: I;
As Cat'lic is, just ere he calls: "to die!";
Retains that mind—ib-ign'rant id-insane,
By ego's title: "God, that he doth ain!"
Descries by bible: action, truth, and lie;
With page once writ by whom, prophetic psy',
While 'nnouncing voice of psy's—are evil, bane.

"'Tis but thy name, that is my enemy,"
For loves the suff'ring pain of Christ with glee;
'N' e'er calls women, "slave, adulter'r, bod'."
To worship men supreme, doth mut'ny God.
What is religion? Power, guilt disguis'd.
"Call thee but love, and I'll be new baptiz'd."

Eo: "early; primeval." Ib: "previously," thus "ib-
ign'rant: "repetitive, stagnant." Ig: "(psychoanal.): "the part
of psyche that seeks satisfaction with pleasure principle;
compare ego."

76

Masters' Lesson: CII {102}

Prayer—should close with word, *Amin,*
(the Hebrew word for *trustworthy*).
Amen— was re'rranged for "group."

"Can't-os" IX: "Hole-y" Land

The sep'rated churches, dissecting God,
Like greedy hyenas, gnawing on bod':
This bit of earth, that bricked-up church;
One soul out of many, just one book search.

Isn't God immense, a universal whole?
Like blind on el'phant, men feel for control:
"The tail is a rope; The ear a *fan-/-see*;
The trunk a snake." All see what want to see.

If Earth and Heavens are God's creat'd feat—
Then ev'ry site is sacred, not one spot;
All wisdom God's mind—not just what taught.
As holy means hole, else spelled wholly, complete.

"*Devil*" and "*evil*" are "*lived*" and "*live*" reversed:
'Tis ruling souls through past action rehearsed.

Lanterns of Caterpillars:

English writes, "Satan,"
but pronounces truth, "sate in":
wrong to stagnate mind.

Masters' Lesson: CVII {107}

If one believes God created universe,
but does not know e'erything un'verse contains—
one cannot know God; merely depths of ego.

STAINED GLASSES

Churches like to preach
"let in— the light of God";
by windows—either stained, or very small.
Thus, their words—are spoken in 90% darkness.

Masters' Lesson: CXCII {192}

Things that possess no power,
no need to fear, condemn, outlaw.
Reason Rome bans books; Druids.

Masters' Lesson: CCXXX {230}

One cannot worship any object—without—
also worshipping God; for it God cre'ted
every living thing in the universe,
then God is in tree; in sun, in cow; in man.

To worship an object, without the image of man, is
to worship that part of God, untainted by man.

Masters' Lesson: CLXXVI {176}

Religions establish prejudice in men,
upholding one adjective o'er another;
yet, many adjectives describe "God," not one.

Masters' Lesson: CLVI {156}

All religions, all men—want a messiah;
but a messiah—who upholds their beliefs.
Men do not want to know God, but own ego.

Masters' Lesson: CXC {190}

Signing cross is cent'ring d'rection's force on self.
ADAM acr'nym for Latin: North, East, South, West.
When changed words, EVE became walking straight narrow,
East-West path from labryinth's coiled serpent-maze.

Labyrinth stems from Latin's "Laborintus." Intus, means "inside." The implication of a labyrinth: "Labor + inside"; "to do one's own spiritual work."

Straight and narrow path": follow men's oughts.

If one has truly accomplished <u>own</u> inner work, there will not be a need to <u>control</u> other men by law and canon; for will have realized the difference between God's intent, and own aiding, by truth.

In *Astronomies & Cultures in Early Medieval Europe* (Cambridge University Press), McCluskey reprints an early church diagram, containing the names of territories (whose first letter's make the acronym of ADAM, in the exact gesture of signing the cross on the body).

Anathole
(Asia Minor; Oriens (East)

Arcton   Mesmbrios
(Aquilo; North)   (Meridie, South)
                    Disis
                    (occidens; West)

Masters' Lesson: XLVI {46}

One can sow same seed—but once.
To reap, one must sow seed of seed.
God did not plant—just one mind.

"So,(sigh), uh, tea?"

Masters' Lesson: CXX {120}

Our bequeathed *deci-*, means *ten*.
One says *decision*, means *tension*.
Ignorance—pressure on mind.

"So, (sigh), uh, tea?"

Masters' Lesson: CCXXXI {231}

Man can't sep'rate his Religion from his State.
Such—asks a soul to d'nounce a part of itself.
Separation of Religion & State means:
Do not display pers'nal view from position.

(Matthew 6:18 "...your father sees you in secret...")

Masters' Lesson: CCXXXII {232}

Nothing so inferior, as to assume,
that anything small or brief—is trivial.
Prepositions indicate "pre-position";
Predetermine character, relationship.

The motto of Washington, D.C.: *Justitia Omnibus* ("You-stit-E-ah Ohm-knee-boos") [Latin: "Justice <u>To</u> all"].

All our laws, then, speak through the word "*to*" (towards). {*To* should not be equated, nor confused with same definition of *"for."* *For* means "suiting the purposes or needs of."}

Justice <u>to</u> all—means laws <u>**affecting**</u> all— but speaks nothing of the benefit <u>for</u>.

Masters' Lesson: CCXXXIII {233}

The most important part of democracy—
is not to be self-centered, and self-serving—
but to be self-governed, and self-disciplined.

"So,(sigh), uh, tea?"

Masters' Lesson: XCVIII {98}

Beware of one who needs power o'er others.
Need for power—denotes insecurity.
Need for power—but serves the self, no one else.
Power is word *owe*, smothered between *P. R.*

Masters' Lesson: CXXII {122}

Pol'ticians with cru'l, thin lips,
with no sensitivity points,
speak sparse of compassion, care.

Lips accustomed to forming—
harshness or softness of the soul.
Lips shape the tone one's spoken.

("The U.S. 2nd Circuit Court of Appeals affirmed a trial court's decision, in favor of the Vermont Department of Motor Vehicles (against P. Perry's vanity license plate, "SHTHPNS")—saying, 'The State has a legitimate interest in not communicating the message—that it (deems to be) offensive scatological public display on State license plates.'

...Perry argued in her appeal...the DMV allowed other vanity plates bearing scatological terms...cited such examples as "POOPER."

The Court wrote: '...the difference between Perry's plates and most of those listed...they do not use easily recognizable profanities... The relevant difference between "S—T" and "Pooper"...the fact that "S—T" is a profanity."

—Reuters 10/20/01)

State of "Amen-duh-meants"

Men may in vain, proclaim profanity—
Even denounce, as trounce, "Insanity!"
Despise dispute, refute humanity—
For 'mendments: no interments on entity.

Thus frantics to semantics of soci'ty,
Need vanity doused with sobriety:
A word's an indiv'dual's identity;
And State—reflected in indemnity.

To thrust and "Perry"—"laud" on contemplate—
Of "fee-seize" "sue-pression"—is censorship.
The language, tongue, is not a "medal" template.
Has R'public "traited" to dictat'rship?

A "def'ni-shun' on freedom's nyms—restricts;
Confined in "what is"—limit has been fixed.

————————————
Medal, meddle.

"So,(sigh), uh, tea?"

Masters' Lesson: CCXXXIV {234}

'Lected man—unfaithful to spouse (vow'd 'fore God),
will be unfaithful to constituents, too.
Proven selfish interests—are prior'ty.
By infidelity—proven he will "lie."

Masters' Lesson: CCXXXV {235}

Ballot should allot vote to vacate pos'tion.
Term vacancy—cannot ruin a country.
Ruined morals—rescind" soci'ty to d'cay.
Vote to vacate must be its constituents.

"So,(sigh), uh, tea?"

Masters' Lesson: CIX {109}

In a reply, the man whose voice nods one way,
while silently shaking his head the other,
is not telling the truth, or states has conflicts.
Silent gesture, always intuitive truth.

[Men are not conscious of head-shake;
therefore do not attempt to manipulate it.]

Masters' Lesson: CCXXXVI {236}

N'er 'lect a man, who cannot write his own speech.
His inept'tude states incap'ble of logic;
Does not contain the ability to think.

Language is the beginning of all thinking.
And thinking—is the beginning of all law.
If one cannot write well, one cannot think well.

"So,(sigh), uh, tea?"

Only when presented
with choice of two ideal candidates,
may one presume—there is no obligation to vote.

Masters' Lesson: CCXXXVII {237}

Emotion cannot be felt by another.
Only aroused by content, delivery.
It's a tool to uphold one's selfish int'rests.

Volume—the imminent, psychological compensation—
that diverts attention to disguise the lie.

Masters' Lesson: CCXXXVIII {238}

A pol'tician too polished, practiced 'fore mirr'r,
to control revealing what he truly is.
One who does not need position to prove self—
will exude comfortable, fluid grace, speech.

Rule of Thumb: "Gov-urn-meants"

What need, have hearts or souls, for governments?
Who're crisp, like parchment, stained, but unrepent.
 To prove upon the page, but n'er in the mind,
 'Tis apathy gained, while wisdom undermined.
  Can lawyer understand the farmer's glen?
 Or fathom teenage-mother's angst and fear?
  A lawyer's educated in law, not men,
  Why law's in'ffective in changing sphere.

 Who can know what another's will may be?
 Each will and dream change in day's subtlety.
  Yet, men try to vent their minds upon men;
Makes slaves of eyes and lives, of mount and glen.
What need have minds, have souls, for governments.
 'Tare men who need control, o'er dimes and sense.

  We are not the "melting pot of the world." We
are—where the world has come to dream. And what dreams
do we give it—if we but seek to enact nightmares?
   The problem is—we believe that others' morals and
solutions affects our own dream. (This is only true, when
made into law.) This is why souls fight, and have fought,
desperately, for so many centuries. In so short a lifespan,
afraid, "will not be able to attain the dream, the soul
desired." The question is, Like Tzu's butterfly, is life—e'en
our own dream?

"*Lie, Sons! Lie*"

Of rid'lous thoughts that man of man demands,
  By far exceeds in lead, the license *Freud,*
    A mentally practicing "hem-ore-hoid,"
    Demeaning ind'vidual self-command.

    To dictate cut of hair, by reprimand
(As though bowl on head, were death employed;
  Or hair, if frizzed or singed, is life destroyed),
    Believes one cannot judge a cut *offhand.*

    This merry-go-round is re*petit*ous.
      Petit is small, making obnoxious.
    Men have no need for paper to approve;
    Discourse in service, will wear its own groove.
    The license but gen'rates money for State,
    To pay man'gement costs of lice'sing debate.

Masters' Lesson: CCXXXIX {239}

Nothing is 'out of context.'
'tis but one's own thoughts—highlighted—
to mirror—shape of one's soul.

Misinterp'tation exists—
as one exactly lettered word,
carries sev'ral def'nitions.

("Action means more than words...")

Masters' Lesson: CCXL {240}

One thought is more valuable than action;
as thought—is the action which seeks solution.
E'en emotion—is analyzed by the mind.

If a question can only be answered "yes" or "no,"
the question is trivial—
to one's growth.

Roman Numeral phonetics: "Seize Excel."

Masters' Lesson: CCXLI {241}

Far harder to sacr'fice brain cell to wisdom,
than sacr'fice body 'pon a bullet, or sword.
Pain of sword onl' felt once. Pain mind thousandfold.
When mind's int'llect exhaust'd—fist it's last resource.

"So,(sigh), uh, tea?"

Llanterns of Caterpillars: Strength

People confuse self.
Think arrogance, strength—same trait.
Strength does not condemn.

Masters' Lesson: XXV {25}

A strong man—has no master;
nor is he a master, himself.
True strength—is ease with all life.

Abraham Lincoln at Gettysburg

-Harrison D. Mason

A silence there expectant, meaning,
and then a voice clear-pitched and tense;
A thousand hearers, forward leaning,
were in the thrall of eloquence.

He saw the graves of heroes sleeping,
He saw men's eyes suffused and dim;
A triumph great, a nation weeping,
Found true expression there in him.

Not often in a nation's story,
such words supreme, such manhood fine;
He gave that day our grief and glory
the dignity of things divine.

Brief, so brief—the words were falling
ere men had time to note and weigh;
as if again the gods were calling,
from some Homeric yesterday.

No impulse this, no actor speaking,
of thoughts which came by happy chance;
the man, the place, were God's own seeking;
the words—are our inheritance.

A pause, a hush, a wonder growing;
a prophet's vision, understood.
In that strange spell of his bestowing,
they dreamed with him, of Brotherhood.

Mentor's Proxy: Gettysburg
[How much we change with just a few words.]

A silence, ere expectant _mean_-ing,
and then a gun, clear-pitched and tense;
A thousand screamers, forward-leaning,
were in the thrall of eloquence.

They paint the graves of heroes sleeping;
they paint men's eyes suffused and dim;
What triumph great, o'er dead mouths weeping.
The true expression: men are grim.

Too often in the human's story,
is anger called _supreme_ and _fine;_
And dares call "day o' grief," a glory!
Death's dignity by war divine!

Brief, so brief—bullets scream'd felling,
ere men had time to note and weigh;
as if Cain and Abel were brawling,
from ancient praise of yesterday.

All impulse this, no human thinking,
wise thoughts to end in humane stance.
The rage, the place: revengeful seeking;
the pain—is our inheritance.

A pause, a hush; resumes the crowing:
red death's vision: riddance good;
In that d'ranged gift of their bestowing,
they dreamed, with Cain, of Brotherhood.

Who's Left[ist]; Who's Left[us].
{In these years, politically alee,
'tis the arts and souls—who suffer the seize.}

Were poets to hold office,
they would only war with wit.
Were filmmakers *"posted in,"*
they would *"fest"* with "picture it."

Were painters forced to convene,
they would shoot a paintball gun.
And singers, armed with precious lyre,
would bow to the golden tongue.

But such souls would mock with glee,
if they supervised the lands;
for know those who start a war,
n'er dirty their dirty hands.

We'd much rather indulge men's thoughts,
painting souls with hues of dreams;
allowing all to best the realm,
with soft and lively, laughing scenes.

Armies! would be the artists!
Banned together to soothe the soul.
And if the tempo be UPRISING!
There would be no obedient control!

Nary would a tax be wasted.
Only the willing allowed to give.
The Endowments would be the focus—
for feeds the soul its "new-trish" to live.

Toiling—would be mirth of dancing!
With soft ribbons and <u>roses</u> aflutter.
Our fam'ly of humans would merr'ly feast!
as we pluck the last soul from the gutter.

But—'tis the shallow and the narrow—
who preach from the<u>se</u> <u>'lected</u> dells;
and they would rather take your money—
to kill diff'rent thoughts and shells.

So—slowly the poets and painters die;
their souls sullen and bereft.
Unhappy in these killing fields,
they crack't ope their shells, and left.

Who is left, but the Weeper and the Reaper,
mentality that makes us weaker.
Who has left? The Deeper of the Keeper,
that were our souls' and future's seeker.

Masters' Lesson: CCXLII {242}

Gove'ment whose upmost concern is ec'nomics,
is a self-absorbed corp'rate monopoly,
whose int'rest is for surv'val of the comp'ny.

Such gove'ment, is barn'cle on society,
leaching for its own use, under the pretense,
of doing for men, what men do for themselves.

Dominion Minion of Opinion
{Beware: word *belief* contains *lie*.}

Every great campaign,
has its nemesis to blame;
to divert attention,
from truth unmentioned.

[Minion: a servile follower; subordinate]

Masters' Lesson: XXIV {24}

Domination—is a fear
within one's self, hoping to hide—
by false show of aggression.

Masters' Lesson: CLXXVII {177}

Fear stems from self-assessment.
As soul cloaked, cannot know other,
onl' past poss'bil'ties of self.

~

"People who think they have superior weapons,
always find reasons to test them."

"Tradition is not sacrosanct;
a bad tradition must be set aside,
and a better one established."

"'Bodies!' Brian interrupted.
'You're talking of conquering bodies!
And I'm trying to make you see the value
of conquering men's hearts and minds.'"

"The king must be the foremost respecter of the law,
even when it goes against him;
or his very land will turn lawless around him."

~

—Morgan Llywelyn
Lion of Ireland

A Note To Society

{After watching *The Shawshank Redemption*}

All men are prisoners, prisoners to life;
shackled in gravity's cuff, in flesh and strife.
All men live behind bars—in *"steel"* thoughts cajole,
for each man's body—a dark, sol'tary hole.

All men are prisoners, doing imposed *time*,
where freedom is the illusion, one but mimes.
Here, each man's conscious—is his prison guard;
there he plans his life's labor—easy or hard.

This ear'th is a labor camp, a prison *sell*;
"a-ccost" clamp'd on chain-gangs' minds—tolls Hell's cartel.
This labor of scraps, for tokens and pension,
'tis mere beggars' dance for fiddler's attention.

Mere ruffians are we! Hardened criminals!
who do not live by love—but codes and penals.
We seek accomplices, who aide and abet,
our cloak of demeanor: *"cost-tomb"* of habit.

Build penitentiaries within this prison;
punish the hurt, the pained, the void of reason.
To these, of our hearts, we choose not to bestow,
but smother, by cement coffin, cru'lly slow.

Man believes himself to be Judge and Jury,
yet, does judge by incompetence and fury.
Attempts to separate himself by *degrees*,
as though he were not the same prisoner he sees.

All souls live under *The Eminent Sentence.*
The unison here, is to seek acceptance.
Onl' God is The Warden, who pardons our curse,
lifts us from isolation of fleshen burse.

Our time is reduced, extended, completed,
when have answered Sphinx riddle—ears deleted:
What is it—one must seek and learn?
State the only jewel—precious to earn.

{Man writes precious as "pre-see-i.o.u's".}

{Hi-Diddly-hoe, I am the fiddler freed of woe;
strumming yon strings of red stained grass—
in mirages of clouds that come to pass.

Listen to the roar of this colorful wine,
Come taste the palette, on which I dine:
Freedom is a choice—made in the mind;
Onl' payments—are smiles—of strangers unkind.}

"To Sentence"

A writer—*sentences* the mind.
A judge—sentences the body.
One—seeks an improvement.
    The other—ekes re*form*.

To solve—is to adjudicate.
To absolve—is to educate.

"So,(sigh), uh, tea?"

Masters' Lesson: LXXII {72}

Anagram of *sue* is *use:* acc*use* others—
of puppeteering choice; yet *use* 'gins with *us.*
One cannot sue other, without suing self,
for partic'pation of accepting belief.

122

"So,(sigh), uh, tea?"

Masters' Lesson: CXXXIV {134}

Injury conduce *jury*.
Incites subconscious to blame, sue.
Accident releases blame.

Masters' Lesson: CCXLIII {243}

Phys'cal structure of bench—not to place higher—
than position of those who stand before it.
Justice blindfolded: Court not need see, but hear.
Same floor position: "ruling can be 'commplished."

"A lost limb, he'd read recently...could nowadays be worth three million dollars in damages...He pictured his daughter's pale face...What fine experts they must be, he thought, to quantify the cost...

...Only a sensible person would be fool enough to (ask)...whether the girls were negligent in riding on the road that morning, and whether the truck driver was negligent in hitting them. Instead, of course, everybody was suing everybody: the girl's health insurance companies; the truck driver; his insurance company; the haulage company in Atlanta; their insurance company; the company that the driver had leased the truck from; the manufacturers of the truck's tires; the county; the mill; the railroad.
No one had yet filed suit against God for letting it snow,
        but it was still early days."

—Nicholas Evans
The Horse Whisperer; pg. 108-9

Masters' Lesson: CXVII {117}

We select and direct the paths we create.
If angry at position in, angry at
having subordinated to diff'rent choice.
Future not past, unless—continue same choice.

To practice the same action—
we but remain "past tense."

You are the Soul—
And the Words Digested.

{Wisdom—is not *relative* to age,
but to coined words accumulated.}

Be careful what you feed your mind.
You stunt your growth on words unkind.
As beggars eat—trash infested,
so the soul—on words digested.

For words make thoughts; can elect to kill.
Some thoughts infect, can make you ill.
Some words can hurt, will keep in pain,
know they're in, when come out again.

What words do you let in so blind?
Be careful what you feed your mind.
Words are uttered from masked souls,
so be careful who you get to know.

Be careful what you feed your mind.
You wound your soul on words' design.

"So,(sigh), uh, tea?"

Masters' Lesson: CXIV {114}

Words are the hands of the soul;
aired, they caress the depths of one.
Their grip can heel, heal, he'll, hell.

128

Llanterns of Caterpillars: Crudity

Crudity's the first
form of ugliness in soul;
unmasked by the words.

Masters' Lesson: || {2}

With one foot chained to the past,
you move only one step ahead.
No farther can your mind walk.

An Ann-a-gram
{I jest, " *Tennos*, anyone"}

Dismembered embers of me remembered,
Contained therein thy thoughts, now got when sought;
Beyond the idle why-not of what-naught,
Is not the dust of me left in that word?
To remind thee to remember what heard?
For thine eyes criticize speculation,
And miss't the truth in interpretation,
Should mind not retrace, when by "oddor" lured.

There's much more to me, and much more to word.
Like son*net*hides *ten*, lest thee see to seek,
Enlightenment may take more for the weak,
But lay there for reasoning, rest assured.
Yea, much more beholds, belies to mere /,
Than *eye* see amid blind tryst to what lie.

–––––––––––––
"Tennos" is "sonnet" spelled backwards. Oddor is odor as
odder: "sense something's wrong."

Nomenclature:
What <u>Lies</u> Beyond Damask Covers

In what's a name? the Bard *"sow posed"* in pain;
But name to shell doth smell a'justed tell.
Much lies in depth to shell of any name!
Mere spell of *shell* e'en states: *sell hell*, the shell;
A *mirage: my-/-rage*, at age so flask
In image (*I'm-age*) speaks but candid truth—
Of *what is in a name*, beyond damask
Covers, what one cannot see blind, forsooth!
To *name*, itself, is *mane* that crowns thy head,
To suggest what rules foremost in thy soul;
Contained therein beyond the title said,
Echoes in words elic't from mindful dole.
Mayhap, be thy name, that o'errule thy soul.
No matte', 'tis all in name, thy truest goal.

Rune's Ruin: A Rued Rude

How men rue another might ruin name!
(Yet, each comprised of three, and few the same.)
Embark upon a path to 'stroy, denounce,
For mind's irritation at last name's ounce,
(As if name defines on all, an act announce;
Is it a greater good, the need to renounce?).
An act a man may cast, when giving shame,
Professes louder, his name hath uglier claim.

How many hours, do men, in squalor waste?
(For shells ablasting echoes, powder'd-holler haste.)
The man of cloth to daughter, pregnant young.
The man of law to brother, words hard-flung.
Ah, only Mary is the womb of worth.
Though Jesus be a bastard, his name's not berth.

{Berth [implying "wide (why'd) berth"]: to give space
to, separate from.}

People who spend their life, *"dwelling"* upon the skin—
have a depth of less than $1/32^{nd}$ of an inch.
Hence, they perceive e'erything in fractions, divisions.

Masters' Lesson: CCXLIV {244}

Men divulge assumptions of an adjective,
based on another's prior experience,
and define own future by that assumption.

Realization is—that all encounters,
all exper'ences are with indiv'dual;
not the collective—of defined adjective.

Masters' Lesson: CCXLV {245}

Those who define, worship themselves by the shell,
are eccentrics; uncomprehensive to truth.
Eccentric: "ec-" ("out of, beyond") + "center."
A mere adjective bleeds the mind from the soul.

"I was born an American;
I live an American;
I shall die an American;
and I intend to perform the duties incumbent upon me,
in that character—
to the end of my career."

—Daniel Webster

"So,(sigh), uh, tea?"

In the midst of alienation—arises an Alien nation.

A "Culture's" Time Spent

Amazing! a *"cult-your"* can RUSH to war!
With speed, without hesitation, kill!
And offer no regret o'er slaughter's ill;
For words *ruse* emotion, from war to "wore."

Amazing! a *"cult-you're"* can RUSH to judge!
With twelve Apostles new, *"a-courting"* death;
Within a few hours, can take a man's breath,
From the'rized thought on speculated grudge.

Amazing! that *"cult-of-inure"* takes YEARS!
To change belief, they don't comprehend,
But do espouse as truth, to bitter end;
Believes the sphere's purpose for fere, *ore* fear.

So Darwin was wrong; Man is raised by words;
We're not compet'ive, but repet'ive *"were'ds."*

Masters' Lesson: LIV {54}

There are no minorities.
There is only thought—which includes,
or excludes—path to one's heart.

Masters' Lesson: CXCIII {193}

If one can't judge any man, situation,
without pointing, 'lluding to pigmentation
(or gen'tals)—one's prejudice; creates tension.
There exists no thing, but thought: manifests all.

Masters' Lesson: LXXIII {73}

Anger, o'er one's words, conveys:
great respect for one's opinions;
else, would not care to try change.

Masters' Lesson: LXVII {67}

Violence is an attempt—
to remove anger from one's mind,
and place it in another.

If one refuses to fight,
one refuses other's anger,
preferring own peace within.

"So,(sigh), uh, tea?"

Masters' Lesson: LV {55}

Respect—is formed by the mind.
Courtesy—is formed by the lips.
Lips define shape of one's heart.

Race: A Contest

{A poet notices skin pigment—
like others notice hair color, and iris hue.
Neither affected, nor impressed by the shell, but the soul.}

I see eyes that invite me in;
of compassion, or curiosity's grin.
Or I see eyes that shut me out,
suspending me in ignorant shout.

I hear voices that are pleasing and mild;
souls aloft, in bliss, undefiled.
Or I hear voices that are harsh and blame;
accusations imbuked for what retain.

I've n'er been simple, as to perceive,
anything shallowly, which deceives.
Should I convey, a manner of hate,
'tis action, not tot'lity, berate.

'Tis tone in voice, the look in eye,
your uneasiness as I walk by.
'Tis dismal face, a lack of smiles,
a "syndication" of defiles.

Ah, I've n'er been simple, as to perceive,
man is made by shell, not ere birth's eve.

Temperament of "Dis-position"

This be true,
we ne'er do,
hate a person.

We learn to hate,
the ingrate
of assertion.

Masters' Lesson: LXXXIX {89}

Descriptive use of word, *race*,
challenges minds to prove the skin,
vies eyes to top, trample soul.

Aphesis

{The gradual disappearance, or loss, of an unstressed,
initial vowel, or syllable.}

To ease our fears, of stingy shares *{allay}*;
We assign value to metal *(alloy)*.
Divide portions amongst ourselves *(allot)*.
Cast votes to redistribute funds *{ballot}*,
Then judge those who use the money *{mallet}*;
Do battle—to shield ideas *{sallet}*.
Allay, alloy, allot—by ballot, mall't;
'Tis but *small change*—by *petty* cash.

What dost gradu'lly disappear *{alter}*;
Unnoticed by aph'sis' action *{palter}*.
Slowly, the chastise of words, harm *{falter}*;
Become *Statute o' Satisfaction {altar}*.
Alter by *palter,* tolls *falter's altar:*
And we worship misery of mankind.

Llanterns of Caterpillars:
A Man is His Words

Rise up by your words.
All man owns—is named by things.
Thus, success is words.

The immenseness of a soul—
cannot be determined by "common cents."

"So,(sigh), uh, tea?"

Masters' Lesson: LXI {61}

A piece of gravel—is same as piece of gold.
Yet, gold is *valued*—because others want it.
Therefore, what's valued—are others' thoughts, not things.

Masters' Lesson: CXLVII {147}

The page of money—is time already spent;
   thus, it can be gambled, frittered easily.
'Tis leisure of future, we don't gamble with.
[What _change_ are willing to make for our future?]

Masters' Lesson: IV {4}

Trinkets adorning the shell—
fill gaping holes in shallow souls,
who cannot contain life's worth.

Masters' Lesson: CXCIV {194}

Clothes reaffirm one's current mentality.
When tire of that garment, one's tired of that thought.
Better thoughts: better quality clothes (lasts years).
All "wardrobes" should be replenished with new, wise.

Masters' Lesson: CI {101}

Gifts giv'n, for audience eyes,
are not about *giving* at all;
but strive to 'prove self-image.

26 alphabetic letters, 9 notes of music.
That man can take the most ordinary, and rearrange
it, so that it is never common compilation—is proof—
that life is never boring.

 'Tis inability to envision creation.

Master's Lesson: CCXLVI {246}

Suffix strips notation from fullness 'fore it.
One's either something, or not ('noted by noun).
Affixing suffix—stip'lation: one is less;
Abil'ty—d'termin'd by mental'ty, not shell.

Masters' Lesson: XIV {14}

Prostitution but implies—
one's naught to offer soci'ty—
but use of shell. What of soul?

Masters' Lesson: LXXI {71}

Complaint o'er others' clothing:
grievance of own sexual thoughts.
Clothes not puppeteer of thoughts.

Masters' Lesson: CXXIII {123}

Word *future* declares *"few sure."*
Go a<u>head</u>, do what you dream of.
No one can know its outcome.

"Few sure" assess onl' money,
predict by others' trail blazing.
Money doesn't control soul.

The Halls of Eternity

The Most Precious Gift

More precious jewels, I could not want,
    than two eyes that gleam adoration.
No shallow things, as trinkets and rings,
    could e'er compare to thy elation.

More valu'ble art, I'd not collect,
than light touch warmly brushed on my soul.
No softened Monet, could e'er display,
    Hued emotion impressed by thy tole.

Of more rare carats, I do not dream,
    than red lips clearly shaped by desire;
and how hard thee kiss, with tender bliss,
weighed by depths of thy passionate fire.

A more lovely cloth, I do not need,
    save for the silk bareness of thy soul:
A pre-designed part, worn o'er my heart,
    of thy warm sheer breath draped to loll.

More mounds of green, I do not require,
    than frolicking lush acres to roam.
Where One hearts build, 'structed timbre filled,
    with enchanted love, to make house *home*.

More prized treasures, I could n'er amass,
than little gems _facet_'d in thy hue;
For when great love grows, it overflows,
and can n'er be contained in just two.

Yea, these, the most precious gifts I seek,
such heavenly treasures should abound!
Yet, aspire for, I'm wretchedly poor,
as the soul I seek—cannot be found.

Masters' Lesson: LXVI {66}

Big diff'rence between use of words: fire, or flame.
Fire cites *ire*: rage in passion, mired by façade.
Flame flutters higher towards *aim, alms,* and *am*.

The Profession of a Marriage Ring

Do not e'er think so little of my love,
To give to me a diamond band, or gold.
Aren't diamonds cut to fit another's mold?
Dispassion'd color? Holding one above?
What men will kill o'er, take life and splendor of?
So hard, di'mond's pain, but cuts ten-fold;
And gold, 'tis ill for man's foolish hold:
A fals'fied lust, o'er surface yeller y'u've."

Adorn my heart with _lustrous_ _copp_er ring,
That metal echoes virtue prom_ising;_
By anagram of _open cope_, declares:
No dream is small; can handle all with care.
For copper is conductor mess'ging through:
_Wh__ere__'er we may be, pulsing love to you._

A Wedding Day Vow

{To be spoken with loving hands, forming a crown,
   placed on thy love's head, emphasizing noun.
and n'er shall thy hands, leave that blushing grace,
e'er throughout the vow, softly caressing Love's face.}

With this heart, avow, I to thee do wed;
And place a wreath of love, around thy head.
Let my love—e'er polish—thy cheeks and eyes;
May they shine with brightness, profess the size;
To show how I cherish, thy heart and soul,
That I may n'er neglect, or dull thee so.
Throughout this life, my love is onl' for you.
Knelt upon my soul, I profess this true:

I honor—thy lips of love, thy soul in eyes.
I honor thy happiness, cherish thy sighs.
I vow to thee, that I respect thy thoughts;
I vow to strive to keep—this blush I brought.
A ring's too harsh, too small for love to know.
This vow is the *cymbal*, that honors trow.

(People worry if a ring isn't worn, spouse will commit
adultery. If a ring is a warning sign to prove, to show—then equates
"no trust." Simply about surface, how things look.)

A fortiori:

An Ode To Hearts, Blushing Empyreal Dreams

That word, love, is pitiful—
in compar'son to how I feel;
it lacks in breath and vibrance,
Heaven's romantic ideal.

{It is mere, shallow, vain.
What others prate, like rain.
'Tis beneath us, of low quatrain.}

Let me not say *"I love you,"*
the way Frops narciss' the word;
and grate incessant use of it,
'til no more meaning can be heard.

Let heart press wildly to heart,
and bruise through a delicate oath:
tapping on chest in Morse code—
how devotion craves us both.

Let my touch, then, spill sight and taste,
a palette of blissful senses;
not where one leaves one alone,
subst'tuting oration, hences.

Let such confess—how I love you;
as that word—that word—cannot bear,
in all its imagined exuberance,
what august breath we share.

{Earth words vainly grasp to breathe,
n'er el'quent to 'qual Hea'en's touch;
And dictionaries—are "tombs,"
where Death is sage—on life and such.}

[Oral "love you's": clumsy, dull, and chored;
See words hide—a double-edged sword,
and can slay, with those bitter flat chords.]

'qual = equal.

A Public Kiss—Long in Yearning

In a room full of sternly held hearts
(those starch romantic *stays*! with *urnest* cold parts),
who, given public displays, would never dream!
(for love, and its need, they deem obscene).

Should I forget *"they're-there!"* at tiring care,
and see only your soul—beyond all compare;
and (k)nee'd to embrace—your kissable face,
cling palms to cheeks, in heart's ached pace.

Should minutes faint by—'neath lips tender plantings,
forgotten the etiquette—of protocol's 'mandings;
ask none of me repent! affection spent!
Importance! I have said it all.
Ignoration—is a cold protocol,
and I *owe-bay* *"a more"* etiquette of truth,
than a pomp mind preached from the book of *Ruth.*

Ah, great etiquette—I must profess—
demands lips be adored, when they beg a kiss,
and abandon all—for that sake, that bliss!

All stolen moments—is this life from Heaven.
Is not much time, aft time found lover.

Love's Embrace Doth Endure

The soft flesh of thy *"mask'line"* cheek,
draped on breast, but profusely reeks,
of love's sweet aroma in "si*(gh)*-lents."
I've no need, but thy breath and scent.

I bury my face, in thy silken waves,
breathe musky scent: how mind behaves;
while thy warmth exude, in airy quip,
but bends soft kisses from my lip.

An embrace in love—it doth endure,
and knows no time, or space, nor cure.

Immortally Married

I don't need my eyes to see you;
as if I were a sense of one.
Though appear one heart beating,
I am but half—a creation.

My ears—burned by flames of your voice,
hear you breathing a world away;
When you utter a mere soft sigh,
'tis thunder! like 'lectric in May.

I don't need my eyes to *seize* you,
though I've never beheld your face.
O'er centuries, o'er galaxies,
over distance of time and space—
I have always walked within you,
which naught can sep'rate, or erase.

"Dear...

"I must write you a line—to sweeten your dinner!
...that my eyes, and lips... You know not how much ten-
derness...may escape in a voluptuous sigh... let not the
light see; I felt it in your arm—hush!...I may drop a kiss
with it (this letter) into your heart, to be embalmed—till
we meet, closer..."

Love..."

{Mary Wollstonecraft to William Godwin}

The Lost Art of A Love Letter

Where is blood from soul, dying *parchment* slips?
A thousand ached praises, on puckered lips?
Impeccably draped, in eloquent adorn—
Vying to be worthy of a statuesque form.

Where are eyes, racing page, in pounding rush?
All folly, in giddiness, of secret blush?
Lightly retracing love's caressed stain—
Where heart dripped wound, in passion reigned.

Lost *darling, beloved,* they've bid adieu;
The pen's tucked away—on nursery rimes' shoo!
This modern love's drunk on wheat rendezvous,*
Turning endearment cold—to *babe* and *hey you.*

[*beer, or bar]

"Speak to me of love;
I thirst for it."

[- Alexander Pushkin (Poet) to Anna Petrovna Kern;
September 22nd, 1825]

Love and Live are only separated by a vowe';
thus live becomes love when two wills bend:

$$1 + 1 = 0$$

LAI

What diff'rence between *lay* and *lie*.
Galaxies' polar'ties, say I.

L ie accents self, and self-need, I,
dueled deceit, in <u>dormancy</u> vie.

L ay *"lines"* its cons'ants as 'qual'ty
ends on support in given "y."

So note the soul, who justifies:
not *lay,* but "tin my heart, you *lie.*"

Such love is false, and noted by,
the choice of word, that love is *lie.*

What Flower To Give

If 'tis a flower, thee wish to enfold,
To sing my heart—a perfume waft of love,
Profess without a word—'doration 'bove—
All else, that I'm by far the richest gold;
These bare the soul, and speak how heart is told:
A Periwinkle sighs: 'Two eyes can't resist.'
Tulips softly pucker, 'Shape need kiss't';
While Bleeding Hearts beweep, 'Thy ache, in mold.'

A rose that's red, is ster'l'ly overdone;
The fragrance gone, so commercially bought,
Suggests cliché of simply anyone,
And think 'tis select without much thought.
If love, in flowers, thee wish to bestow,
Then speak such flowers, say my heart thee know.

This Flower, Paper-Prettied

This flower, paper-prettied, that you give,
One cut from life, with but days to live;
What do you give, but death—
As I watch it bleed, its last "daze" of breath.
Better to give me a packet of seeds;
A pot, some soil, and the care it needs.
If flowers are meant to symbolize,
Send me nothing short-lived, pained, or guised.

This flower, paper-prettied, how it holds,
What possessed care for life thou thoughts befold;
To kill a plant, for smiles and flattery,
'Tis false compliment of perfumed battery.
This flower, paper-prettied, it is you—
Unbidden from finery, and blood feigned blue.

The Throes of Rose

The rose, by cue, is placed on coffin chests—
In range of 'motion: *fling, acquaintance, guest;*
Is thrown to strangers, "care'ess" on first dates;
The gift of fools, whose love unhesitates.
A <u>hand</u>k<u>er</u>chief flower, dropped for any dole,
Retrieving folly—mind enslaves control;
Its million adaptations, gives insight—
The love "ahead," does prick "ascented" fight.

For a clichéd love, a cliché rose will do,
For naught in heart, but acting love adieu;
That feigns for crowds, what love once lost, meant to,
And how heart lay in torment—('til 'nother new).

A rose is a million faces in disguise;
If tries to 'fess: *especial love*, it lies!

Especial and *special* hold same definition, except
especial begins with ESP (true knowing).
Care'es: careless.

177

The body is given lightly in lust;
but the heart can only be given in trust..

Modern Love: "Mode Urn L_uh-v"
{Conduct contained, becomes emptiness of death.}

This modern love, is like a mini blind,
when broken, it's viewed "broken complete."
Yet, nothing wrong with slats (the gift to mete),
and nothing wrong with strings (the ties that bind);
the handle turns, the brackets hold, remind—
its frame-work ever strong, unscathed, accrete.
Not seen in frame, a little gear effete,
that's worn from turning fast pace of mind.
But rather than invest a little time,
a little 'pplied effort, and change of sense,
these moderns pitch it, and buy a new rime,
(the distant façade called indifference.)
No one will see—how all these *blinding leers*,
but tox'fy land, with *plastic-razed* veneers.

(We but call them—children of divorce.)

The Kissing Tree

Go, walk your love, hand in hand, o'er meadows,
 And plant a <u>sap</u>ling, in the name of hearts,
 And say with r'mantic eyes, "*our love here starts;*
It shall bloom, at least a hundred years and boughs,
 While symbolizing strength, e'ery passing day;
 Long out-living halven-souls, caught in flesh."
 Around its body, plant a live floral wreath:
Whose blooms would sigh such words from heart as breath.

It shall croon 'pon whispered winds, the music of—
 The soul in silence—that sipp'd the eyes as wine;
 And lived in love—by branching heart's entwined.
 With nectar's scent—states how sweet was love.
 And when in some vibrant *timbre's* abode,
 'Twill softly sing of kisses, love *still* sowed.

Masters' Lesson: CCXLVII {247}

The heart is equal distance from loins and mind.
Love, then, is a balance—of lust and respect.
Letter A—is the balanced symbol of pair.
Heads meet in un'ty; extension built from heart.

Masters' Lesson: Game-Love

Heart draws two ears connecting.
A broken heart is the result,
when one ear stops listening.

Masters' Lesson: CX {110}

Pain oft' feel throbbing in heart—
is not others beating 'pon, but,
love pounding to be released.

Masters' Lesson: In the Head of Lead

Leading partner, symb'lizes life decisions.
Dance partner, leads without asking—forces men.
Dance partner, who asks to lead—sensitive mind.
True partnership, exchange leads, not needing lead.

Sexuality—focuses upon one sense, one organ.
Sensuality—all the senses,
including the mind, and the soul.

Masters' Lesson: LX {60}

To seek emotional truth—
one must listen to one's own heart.
The mind—holds breath of others.

Yeats—Gonne, Maud

{"When his first mature poem, The Wanderings of Oisin, was published in 1889, it brought him a visit from a beautiful reader, Maud Gonne—who said the work had made her weep.

Yeats—remained hopelessly in love with her, until he died."

-Rodney Phillips
The Hand of the Poet}

To aspire in the moment—
a perfume breath of air;
and languish *foray* lifetime—
with unrequited fair;
All for a careful tongue,
who handsome, unraveled there;
does the heart e'er know love?
or infatuated care.

Painted words, do not precious make a pair.

Beauty Is Solely In The Eyes
{Coinage professes "beauty's" key: "be-u-tee."}

Yes, "beauty's in eye of beholder,"
But not inferring it's what one sees.
The key's the eye (*diff'rinse* o' fleshen frieze),
That lures, aspires; what sparkles, smolders.
Cut eyes from any *"poor-trait" "mottled"* folder,
What's left that may of beauty appease?
To prick and perk the flesh's for lacker's seize—
For what is flesh—if eyes are empty holders?
Thus flesh, all flesh, are shrouds of rubber suits;
Mere rise and fall the same, without <u>uni</u>que gems,
As eyes unveil intent, while flesh merely mutes.
It is the look within—where beauty stems.

Beauty—is to "be yourself to a tee."
Without the soul—we *"suit"* in misery.

{What is the face? *Face* and *phase* stem from the
same root word: *Face* from Latin *facies* [appearance];
Phase from Greek *phasis* [appearance]. Implication: "An
inner phase going through."}

"Wee'ds"

~

"Men are generally more careful of the breed
of their horses and dogs, than of their children."

— William Penn

"If we had paid no more attention to our plants,
than we have to our children, we would now be living in
a jungle of weeds."

—Luther Burbank

~

Masters' Lesson: LI [Lie] {51}

Family is but short for fam(liar)ly:
envir'ment one's conditioned, accustomed to.
True belonging is that contained in each soul.

Masters' Lesson: LXXIV {74}

A parent cannot give—what does not possess
(such as confidence, self-esteem, and self-love).
The soul must find the courage within itself.

Masters' Lesson: CLXXX {180}

Constant "hand-me-downs" imply:
"one's not good 'nough spend money on."
Will carry that thought all life.

Masters' Lesson: XXXI {31}

Child reflects parents' emote,
and but mimes conduct exuded.
Punish thyself, not the child.

Masters' Lesson: XXVII {27}

Parents who control with force,
are venting their hostilities
of world 'round them, on the child.

Llanterns of Caterpillars:

Man conditions thought.
Blank mind birth, r'presents freedom.
To not seek thought, slave.

Man is the only animal—
who forces his children
to pay him—to eat.

Masters' Lesson: CXLI {141}

From seed, plant in environment acclim'ted.
Quick transplant from environment shocks spirit.
Attentive nurturing ensures survival.
Thus is man; the child, the sensitive seedling.

["Heal" derives from Gothic "hal" meaning "whole."]

Masters' Lesson: CXXXVIII {138}

Of all things we imagine,
how many do enact in life.
Child's imag'nation's no threat.

Masters' Lesson: CXXXIX {139}

An adult can never look at life (or book)
with the same perception, viewing of a child.
(Fire is understood—by burn—not by hearsay.)
Outlook changed by exper'ence—not cur'os'ty.

Innominate: A Nursery Rime

I knew a boy, stubborn of pride.
I knew a girl, full of woes.
They met, soon married, and divorced;
left a wee child in their throes.

In the distance, _cools_ the child's heart;
You may wonder how she grows.
With eyes, vulner'ble and vol'tile,
for Stubbornness and Woes she knows.

To Walk On Stars

Teers: No "Re-Joyce"

I know that I will never see,
an el'gy ugly as that tree.
That tree, whose angry mind is "pressed,"
and robs the heart of many breast.
That tree will mock at God all day,
and lift the heavy heart as prey.
That tree but stretches necks with wear,
infests with bascule "no one cares."
Upon whose needles dreams are slain,
for many mock "you can't attain."
Yes, "Poems are made by fools like me,"
without words—'void errantry.

Bascule: seesaw; derived from French "baculer":
"to strike on buttocks" (punish).

Masters' Lesson: IX {9}

Suicide is the yardstick,
'gainst which collectively measure,
our reflected inner worth.

Masters' Lesson: XXVIII {28}

Like dense barren rock grows plant,
so does the soul—have depth—to grow
fruition out of nothing.

Masters' Lesson: CCXLVIII {248}

To cast off shells—must kill it;
whethe' by ropes, guns, tir'dness, disease.
All del'b'rate—when want to go.

Masters' Lesson: ||| {3}

One life is not important.
Even the winds and rain erode
the vain writing of tombstones.

Masters' Lesson: CLXXIII {178}

A man's only worthy estate—is his heart.
Outer things: material'zation of heart;
bequeathed things, but remind what of heart was giv'n.

Fresh Cuts (Turned Beauty's Bloom)

Bid bye, freshly cut flowers 'pon the grave,
and bloom in Love's hand, in Hea'en's enclave.
Wilt thee, as fading hue's a connection,
where souls can speak, by same sight, affection.

"For my gentle *Sunflo'er,*" she sleeps above.
Long has she been gone, but still so in love.
Let her e'er walk among these *Garden Whites,*
for mem'ries, Love, of *E'ening Blooming* nights.

"I press a kiss, in 'roma's *Lyssum* sweet,"
"Weep soft, *Cathedral Bells,* and chime to sleep."
"Here lays *Baby's Breath,* a sweet and pure cher',
may God keep you warm, and always dear."

Bid sigh, fresh-picked flowers 'pon the grave;
and message to my Love, "piece of soul, I saved."

Cher': cherub.

The "Corps" of Company C

Should they call me to thy bedside,
 with alarm of heart on lungs;
and bade me come to state *goodbye*,
 when barely a hello was sung.

Should they call me to thy fun'ral,
 to mourn and weep for what?
Bade me succumb to solemn eyes,
 in paraphernalia's strut?

I tell you—I will not.

Should I talk when you are gone?
And beg my absence understand?
And gather on avoided hill,
with tongues awringing, like hands?

Should I *rearrange* your corpse,
like the masses who speak for show?
Should I treat you to piece of dirt,
 where esteem'd caste sinks low?

I tell thee—I will not!

Do not call me to a fun'ral,
I can not mourn, or weep, or strut.
I cannot feign a stream of tears—
which but pities selfish gut.

Do not call me to a fun'ral;
what's left to say is naught.
Onl' compan'nship speaks how precious,
but before Death's door is shut.

What is a funeral—but "few-neurals."
Are caskets, then, not "souven-ears?"

Masters' Lesson: CC {200}

Do not have regret for missed apology.
One may miss the person, (momentarily)—
but shall encounter the soul in etern'ty.

Bier Intoxication: Men Drunk on Death

[Stressing, first, its "icks," and "oos!"]

How death makes men euphoric,
    (Deceived by bier, distort the truth),
And claim by monuments historic,
    (Where even flaws, become a noble couth)
That one was perfect, divine rhetoric,
    (For what a swine supposed to be in youth);
Perhaps, "for<u>mal</u>-de-hyde," suffers logic,
    (For ills disappear before eyes, when soused).

This talk's "sincere" (a "sin" embalmed by "wax"),
"Under—taken" faces can n'er hide the facts:
Those kindly words attempt to lessen sass,
Speaks how want treated, when own time comes to pass.

Men spell "death" "dei-th": suddenly <u>di</u>vine.
(P'haps, counting blessing: fin'lly rid of E'stein.)

[What would world be like, if Einstein had never lived,
and never invented the atomic bomb?]

Bier: a frame, or stand, on which a corpse, or coffin is
laid, before burial. Cere: cerecloth (a cloth coated with
wax, formerly used for wrapping the dead.)

Facades Manes

All bones are white,
the flesh, a draped stole.
Succumb in the facade,
shrink and lose the soul.

At twenty-eight, I will not *weight*—
my soul, with Narcissus' deafening Echo.

Manes: the spirits of the dead, in ancient Roman
belief, to whom graves were dedicated. The spirit or shade
of a particular dead person.

216

Siege

Conceit—is the marriage of _con_viction—with de_ceit_.
We only free ourselves, from our self,
trapped in other people—by thought.

{Obsolete definition of _siege_: a seat; man-made
distinction; a throne.}

Atrophy's Trochee Touché

{"Queen Noor watched her husband's burial from afar... Muslim tradition prohibits women—even wives—from attending burial rites..."

-Repository, A-6, 2-9-99}

Go, and visit graves, undressed as still a man.
Weep, whilst not in presence of scorning wo(o)man.
Mock pretense, pretentiousness, that men don't keep—
Hours and hours of pain, of heartaches stif(f)led deep.

Go, and visit graves, while dressed as still a man.
May be last time, shall have the priv'ledge 'gain.
Graves but come acalling, all too soon undon,
Striping "sheath" and "sword" humans "focuss" upon.

The question at end (all one's action bade):
If thoughts and feelings instilled—felled men, or aide?
Only men place the higher price on principles,
Leaving hearts and souls behind, as prince's fools.

World's problems, strife, aren't zephyr's bomb, or Zen.
Infer'ness cast—sep'rates man from men.

Trochee: poetic meter of "stressed, unstressed" syllables (Implication: first importance); verses the sonnet's natural meter: "unstressed, stressed."

Llanterns of Caterpillars: The Vain of Vein

Every man has a—
woman's menstrual cycle—
flowing through his veins.

No man can denounce—
he's separate from woman;
vital blood is hers.

Effigy Ephemera: For "Ruse-O-Svelte"

[Adhere † Ad Rem † Ad Padres]

May? Ninety-Seven. (Did three not vote?)
"Heroic deed!" the newsmen wrote.
In honor of— *"Dear F.D.R.,"*
who adv'cated, *help feed the poor."*
A monument, a *"Ruse-so-fied"*
(must due something— seemed glorified);
and so from funds, they fritter-start,
for *erection*—o'er mind and heart.
For *ty-two* point—five million spent,
for *see-man* site, for *hard* cement.
Free tax collect: foolish effuse;
other uses—which we could use.
Like wipe out debt, or homelessness;
or child abuse, or stupidness.
Those very things, which *F.D.R.*—
advocated, and *"stood-up"* for.
Would that not be—great *"monumeant"*:
accomplish tasks, his implements?

May, Ninety-Seven? (A question asked?
A meta*phor,* per*mission* tasked?

If men like *Frank,* had such great verve,
    Why law limit—on term to serve?
    Law of limit—conveys the truth:
Uncs don't admire—compassion's couth.
Our lim'tations—once raised, are razed;
while *"at-tribute"*—what want to praise.
Statues, statutes: pillars of SALT;
    irritation *cites*—blame and fault.
What *"leg-a-cy"*—do we e'er need,
    but one of mind, intell'gence seed.
Perhaps, we need—to plant that seed,
    in mind of those, who favor shows—
o'er feeding poor, and soothing souls—
    through art, music, and po'tic tolls.
    This word I sow:
a monument—can not but grow—
    sorrow's lament.

SALT: Strategic Arms Limitations Talks (or Treaty).
Adhere Ad Rem Ad Padres: stuck to the relevant dead.
Ephemera: anything short lived; thus, statues crumble to
dirt; but without a soul's memory or eternity.

Masters' Lesson: CXLIV {144}

Honor every day of breath—
use fine china, crystal, goldware.
Each day—special occasion.

The Bastardization of Dastardization

How dare a man may choose to selfis'ly die!
That he may decide, he's too good for his disease,
And asks to pull the plug to end his miseries—
Without considering a stranger's eye,
How stranger's affected by suicidal bye;
Or stopping to ask if his act may appease,
Belief of God and pain, so stranger may be eased.
How dare a man may opt to "croak and die!"

The death that men accept is found in war,
Where men can kill men, over dirt and ore;
(Though soldier killed, was saved from abortion,
Can pull a trigger on thought's abhorration).
Who believes the soul belongs to itself;
Mere puppets to play on ego's "ry, belf-."

"Ry, belf: " is "belfry" (idiom: "bats in the belfry";
insanity), scrambled to deduce a screwed-up mentality.

223

Death occurs—when eyes stop dreaming in this world.

Eco, Echo, & Ego

"Laugh-tear"

Unto any situation—reaction is gauged by such:

A tear— is a resignation,
whereby the soul accepts allegation,
and yields all possibilities to defeat.

Laughter—is agility,
gently shakes one from immobility,
to allow one to move to adept feat.

A tear—seeps out the soul,
to quietly vanish unavenged.
Laughter—howls into the wind—
hungry for any challenge.

Masters' Lesson: CCI {201}

Smile—is path that widens souls.
Passed lip to lip, like waves of heart
it clears misery of man.

[Smile calls the lips: "a small aisle"]

Masters' Lesson: CLXXV {175}

I is a "tee," underlined;
drawing gain—begins with one's self.
The tee is the mind and word.

Masters' Lesson: CCXLIX {249}

Man's fear is like a gall stone:
minute discomfort focused on,
whose passing is tempor'ry.

X+Y=G (Goal)

Y is the infinity (endless possibilities) that I am.
X is the ability to cross out action that doesn't work.
Life is the equation of application "why"—
with the solution always seeking—to be greater than I am.

Masters' Lesson: CCL {250}

Can't build man—by first d'grading.
Confidence, strength— built word by word.
Strength comes only from the mind.

The very essence of thought,
is coined upon the opinion, "thou—ought."

Masters' Lesson: CCLI {251}

What fear? R'putation? (Presumptions men incline.)
Death? (Soul r'turning home.) Pain? (Invention in mind.)
God? (We are but the Creator's creation.)
Lack? (Rich in dream and self-esteem produces.)

Masters' Lesson: LXXXIII {83}

Imagine: "Eye-magic-in."
To see power within one's self,
abil'ty to do an'thing.

Llanterns of Caterpillars:
"A-banned-on-Meant"

Men abandon dreams.
Dreams do not abandon men.
Success is time spent.

"Con-tro-verse-ease":

The body, nude, in flesh,
 is considered scandalous.

The body, nude, in paint,
 is admired for it's taint.

The body, nude, in lens,
 sexually offends.

Yet, the body, posed three ways,
 n'er changed through all conveys.

What changed was man's thought:
 each a drape on <u>can</u>vas ought.

Lambdacism:
Has Aubade Degrade to Obeyed?

The only human questions so esteemed,
pertain to work and weather; whether work.
Not happiness, what eyes have seen.
Not sculpted sighs, nor fire of mien.
Not colors, scapes a soul has dreamed.
Not visions, conquest in thought.
Their relativity is apt to naught,
But work and weather, work and whether work.

So I but sigh, of *fiers*, colors dreamed,
Their art so plagued in ètude Bruit-eh?
By souls made sallow on business grey;
For what is made by bus'ness, but dirt esteemed.
Such starch do stop what songs—earl' birds may sing,
Be lawed and 'plaud by laggard's flog for king.

Lambdacism: excessive use of sound, and its
misarticulation. Aubade: musical suite to greet the dawn.
Fier: one who "fies!" (disgust).
Mien: demeanor, showing character. Etude:
musical composition. Bruit: rumor. Etude Bruit-Eh?:
jests: "Et tu, Brute?" (What Caesar uttered to Brutus
before Brutus stabbed him.)

Masters' Lesson: CCLII {252}

Lines on the side of the eyes:
Wincing with unnoble thought.
Emb'rassed by what self often says.

7/7/8

Masters' Lesson: CXXX {130}

Men wish, in vain, to touch sky,
n'er realize sky touches ground.
Life is mirage of thought viewed.

Masters' Lesson: LXXVIII {78}

Space program is symbolic—
of "running away" from problems—
man created on "plan-it."

Masters' Lesson: LXIX {69}

Man's most obstrusive action—
is altering living beings—
to appease invented fears.

All man does—is sell the earth;
as is, or in refashioned form.

Masters' Lesson: CCLIII {253}

Men hang men 'pon m<u>ora</u>lity's conviction;
Always ruling an adjective over truth.
The mind's pursuit of its amelioration,
Spent in silence, seeking answers in own mind.

People do not have conversations—
they have accusations.

Amelioration: become better.

Masters' Lesson: CCLIV {254}

Test of one, 'How long can be alone with self.'
The length of solitude, denotes inner worth.
When one's empty inside, need people around.
(Cannot "stomach" self; Ignore compulsive rot.)

Men have but gossiped—for thousands of years;
and all e'er profess—but ignorance and fears.

To eat with the fingers,
is to honor God,
as God created their beauty.

How Strange This Human Dwelling

They cast names to the winds and disease,
    as if denouncing reality in lieu.
"Oh, looky! Here comes Typhoid Mary!
And, Oh goody! Hurricane Andrew!"

    Let's invite them to tea, shall we?
Embrace them with a champagne toast;
    then dance upon paled sands, with glee,
in mock-wake of Gods and Ghosts.

And with the flick of duality in their face,
    dehumanize drowning souls;
as if to shell-sep'rate their native base—
    from this *Gaudily* mirroring whole.

See out in the "tieds," the tourists' vanity,
    film a woman drowning alone.
She sinks to bottom of inhumanity,
    as if she were no more than a stone.

But, Oh!, well—if she were only a stone—
they would have gladly jumped in to save her.
    A glitter of diamond, ruby, or gold—
what divine lodes! just precious to *savor.*

Here, disease makes money. Dare winds, that's funny!
warhooped emotions—none ease;
for government's gas, strung out on cast—
of anthrax'd, trigger-happy gunnies.

How's death protection? Put on a "con-dumb"—
to annihilate men by the sum.
Here, man's no name, but "numb-ber" insane,
taut to cuddle objects as numen.

Some say man's comprised of two faces inside,
shown in "foe-tow's" left and right view.
These worlds collide, no wonder man's fied,
on compassion and truth of you.

Numen: divine supernatural power, esp. associa-
ted with a particular place or object.

Masters' Lesson: CCLV {255}

Limitation like fly—angrily beating
against window pane; trapped by its decisions.
To release self, fly must travel unknown paths
of darkness, for unknown path led to false light.

Masters' Lesson: CCLVI {256}

Fly on window pane in winter, wanting out.
Yet, fly cannot perceive drastic climate change,
from where fly is at, to where fly wants to be.
Think; fly did not build pane. Who's responsible?

Masters' Lesson: CCLVII {257}

Do not seek to kill fly.
Its death will come in its own time.
The pane it walks on is bread.

Pane: Pan, in Greek, means "all." Ne, in Japanese, means "root.."

Masters' Lesson: CCLVIII {258}

There's no life—not spent in service of others.
All men are servants; regardless of title.
Life's question not—"*What want to do?*" but "How *serve.*"
Life not mult'ple-choice question; but fill-in-blank.

Masters' Lesson: CXV {115}

Palm's lines outline life's desires,
in Sanskrit, Chinese, or Rune marks.
Lines on feet are path shall walk.

Masters' Lesson: CL {150}

<u>A</u>mulets, rings, and tat<u>too</u>s,
but serve as minute re<u>min</u>der
for what is a<u>ready</u> there.

The position on body,
an<u>noun</u>ces weakness in soul, mind;
thus, need for emph'sizing thing.

(CL—means "seal.")

Masters' Lesson: CCLIX {259}

Disabled (handicapped) is spelled "dis-a-bled."
Implies condition results from blocked blood flow.
Leg falls "asleep," can't move. Why? Blood flow missing.
Blood flow, then, equals control of the body.

[If the soul could be proven, it will be proven in
the difference of blood analysis, before and after
"death," when the blood remains, but life force is
gone.]

Llanterns of Caterpillars: Sick

Latin shaped English
Thus, when state *sick*, convey *sic:*
"I am in this way."

Masters' Lesson: XC {90}

Condition of body is—
a manipulation of thought,
oft repeated in one's mind.

Masters' Lesson: CCLX {260}

A thought is the most powerful ingestion.
Neural network in brain, controls the body.
Thus, what assume, has greatest power to kill.

(to Feng Shui)

Masters' Lesson: CCLXI {261}

If exterior disturbs interior,
then the interior is not well designed.
The exterior reflects interior.

Masters' Lesson: CCLXII {262}

A pebble tossed in a pond,
does not alter, or change the pond.
Man—ninety-eight percent—pawned.

Masters' Lesson: CCIV {204}

A pillow is comprised of words *ill* and *ow*.
Remove the pillow, remove the ill and ow.
Head cocked at angle, stresses bones, muscles, heart.

Consumption's Presumption:
"A-sump-shun"

To spend one's life, o' worr'ing over things,
about consumption, fat, a diest spat;
what may kill, what may harm, Dear-God-alarm!
as if from death, one could steal and charm,
a few more years to rot on this whine,
and hope God *merc'flee* forget one in time.
Is Death not Savior from things undivine:
obese obsession, ugliness of mind?

A diet consists of thought and food,
those moral, immoral, polite, or rude.
Whate'er one limits, <u>diet</u> 'gins with die:
'tis lack of pleasure found in <u>life</u>'s sly lie.
Stagnation kills the body or brain;
As death is presumption from what abstained.

{Man writes *food* for *phooe'd*, and *words* for
were'ds. Means his thoughts are the past, and passed is
bought miens. }

{Sump: stomach; nutrient pump; Assumption}

Masters' Lesson: CCVI {206}

Cloning—aesthetics facades to opinion.
Education clones mind to think alike, yet,
few draw the same conclusion; just memory.
God clones: identical twins; clone not android.

Masters' Lesson: *CCV* (205)

No greater authority
on mental'ty of a people,
than its dictionary tome.

How few positives exist.
This is why man writes in "cursive."
It's a style full of "loopholes."

Masters' Lesson: CCIX {209}

There exists no such thing as insanity.
There is only the focus of misery.
One cannot be "out of brain," controls body.
Brain, soul's seat; contains 'cquir'd data, unused, 'til...

Seven:

Se (apart) V (indicator) en (within)

There are a million words in the English language—all coined to support seven: "I like it. I don't like it." Thus, our only concern—is how things impact us.

Man has seven senses. Six in the head (sight, hearing, taste, smell, rational thought, intuition [third eye]) and one—at the end of his fingertips. Touch, then, is merely an extension of the mind;

The soul—is seated in the brain—for all neural network relays back to it.

Se: prefix, meaning "apart."
En: prefix, meaning, "within."

Masters' Lesson: CXLVI {146}

It is not the construction of physical,
but the determination of the mental—
which carries one to the desired heights and goals.

Masters' Lesson: CLXIX {169}

The body can be physically stagnant,
but one can never be mentally stagnant.
To scale another mountain, descent begins.

Disagreements with Feng Shui

Feng Shui believes that though Mountain is a great reservoir of strength, its energy is sapped by plant life, and "weakened" by water.

Nothing conquers Earth, not e'en man.

Plant life—is an extension of Earth. As plant life dies, it produces more dirt, by decaying to what it was before it was formed: more Earth, more Mountain. By this means, Earth conducts growth of its soul, and of its being.

Earth uses its own inner Fire (volcano) to forge parts of itself.

Water cannot damage Earth, for Earth supports water. Without a place to exist, water cannot be.

Earth utilizes water—to continue the growth of its plant cycle, regenerating as Earth.

Air is the aura of Earth, the initial breath, used to cool temperament, and restore balance. (Does man not apply this system of "taking a deep breath" to restore balance of temperament to himself?)

Metal—is Earth reshaped by man—into what opinion man thinks Earth should be—but it is still Earth.

Masters' Lesson: CLVII {157}

A picture of a hero, or an idol,
is but four-hundredth of a second—of life.
Heroes and idols are worshipped in fragments.

Allusion

A seed increases the size of earth,
Mature to plant, decay to girth.
The leaves will shed, and rot away,
The blades are mowed, and turned to clay.
The tree will fall, and ash its mass.
All creatures eat, and excrete pass.
The grains do bloom, and march to see.
Each one once seed, mere dot obeah.

Thus, Earth was n'er one partic'lar size.
But constant'ly growing "orbit-all."
Not worth effort of measuring rise.
Mere metaphor of human mind in sole.

This mass of souls, mast in space,
Is cursed and blessed by "beating grace."

{Do not waste your eyes on what you see; you will
not receive answers, so much as momentary solutions, for we
are constantly evolving.}
Obeah: A belief involving sorcery; magic.

Masters' Lesson: CLVIII {158}

One tree can change the shape of the horizon.
No generation ever sees the same land.
By birth of life, diff'rent perspectives are made.

Llanterns of Caterpillars:
Chaos is Birth Rate

Plant trees together—
and they compete for the top;
"Would" strong; intake small.

Masters' Lesson: XXII {22}

To have evolved full circle,
one learns knowledge of beginning.
Did you need journey—to hear.

Masters' Lesson: CCXI {211}

Does butterfly know what color wings will be,
while still dreaming in the change of the cocoon?
Man's cocoon is Earth, and his color: wisdom.

In the end—
what do any of us have,
except the belief—that we had.

A Pane Defrosted

Two roads diverged in a craven wood,
And sorry the word, I misunderstood;
Appeared before my eyes as "wooed,"
And led astray my "would-be-rood."

I failed to see the aperture:
That anytime, my path's rapture,
Could forge from any given sight,
And not the dictate left or right.

That all along the route did lay,
A three-hundred-sixty-degreed, "which weigh";
Where footing, though difficult and slow,
Would imbue a strength—that few would know.

Two roads diverged in a "would," but I—
Decided I would no longer believe:
Life was two choices, with no reprieve.
(And that, has "maid awl" the "diphy-errands".)

("Maid-awl": someone to make decisions for you,
based on their work; which will make one repeat own lessons.
"Diphy-errands: two-fold tasks.)

Notations:

Llanterns of Caterpillars: Llan, is Welch, for "church." Tern means "three." Caterpillar can be broken into "cater" (serve) and "pillar" (support).

All Llanterns are true haiku meter. 5/7/5.

Master Lessons are worked to higher syllabic division. Either 7/8/7, or lines of 11. 11 is an equals sign in an upright position.

Use of archaic nouns, verbs: man stopped progressing at that point in history.

Excerpts from
Need I Say 'More' (philosophy)
by Ann Marie Yeager:

~

Is there free will,
when men don't think;
but merely side with arguments and adjectives?

~

Without honesty,
one denies others,
the test of their soul.

~

(lie detector test, etc.)
When people accept machinery—
in place of humans—
they will no longer accept humans.

~

Civil Liberty v. Civil Rights

A liberty—
is an infringement
on a right.

~

Politicians who remark "let history" prove my decisions,
do not strategize for the future,
but the past, ever.